Dear God: Passionate Prayers in 140 Characters or Less

Volume 1

(The Power of Words)

@thatwritingchic

Published by Words To Live By Publishing, LLC
Copyright © 2014 by @thatwritingchic
Cover Design: Colleen Piovesan

Scripture quotes are taken from The Message.
Copyright © 1993, 1994, 1995, 1996, 2000, 2001, 2002. Used by permission of NavPress Publishing Group

Printed in the United States of America
ISBN 978-0-9960129-2-8

DEDICATION

I wrote so many versions of this dedication page that I couldn't even decide which to use.

One version thanked my children profusely for being God's greatest gifts to me.

Another version thanked the thousands of Twitter followers who encouraged me to write the book, without even knowing who I am.

Yet another was dedicated to my mother who instilled in me the priceless gift of relationship with God.

But, on March 22, 2014 I deleted all of them and decided to dedicate this book to the memory of Nico Chase.

"Dear Nico: You once tweeted me "If @thatwritingchic wrote a book, I would read it." I didn't even know you were my son's friend at that time. Your replies to my "Dear God" tweets were always heartfelt, genuine and I came to realize more insightful than most young people your age.

I never got the chance to tell you that the book was done and I planned on giving you a copy. I hope you are reading this from your new home in heaven where you can shine the way you were intended to."

For all of the incredibly talented 19 year olds, their family, friends and loved ones who can't begin to comprehend how much God loves you, I hope this helps you understand.

PREFACE

January 27, 2014

Dear God: Thank you for constantly reminding me of the power of words and for each accidentally on purpose moment in my life.

I woke up this morning with the word "determined" heavy on my heart.

Early this morning.

5:40 am to be exact.

If you don't follow me on twitter, you aren't aware that I've been writing "Dear God" as 140 characters or less tweets since 2009.

Even if you know me personally, you may not be aware that I first wrote the words "Dear God" as a very young child.

Yup.

I wrote a letter to God and put it in my window on a very bleak, rainy day.

I took a nap and when I work up, the sun was shining and there appeared the most beautiful rainbow.

I didn't even know the significance of the rainbow at that time!

That cemented my belief in God and the knowledge that he hears and answers my prayers.

The combination of writing and prayer are why I woke up this morning with the word determined in my brain.

For the past three years, I have been determined to compile my "Dear God" tweets into several books.

And each time I got close, the enemy would send a mine to deter me.

First, I struggled with whether or not I should give the books away for free or sell them.

Next, I could not settle on a format that made sense to me.

Then, I felt betrayed by a confidante who knew about my tweets and book.

Two days before my release date, she announced the release of her book with a strikingly similar title.

And when I got access to my entire Twitter archive, I realized I easily had enough content for more books than I could count.

How could I ever decide which content to use?

Deterred by mines.

It wasn't until today that I took apart the word determine.

And I realized that the enemy mines that had been sent to deter me had caused me to be less determined.

Imagine that!

I've self-published three other e-books with no hassle. But, this book is different.

Why?

Because, while I am sharing my personal journey and perspective- it's not about me.

Nope.

It's about glorifying God with my gift.

So, I went away to finally figure out which of the thousands of pages of content I would use.

Imagine that, my very own personal writer's retreat!

Determined to come back with a complete manuscript.

After all, I built the website, and began expanding my reach on Social Media.

I had never gotten that far before. Determined.

And then the enemy sent an even larger mine to deter me.

While away specifically for the purpose of getting the book done, I slipped and fell.

And as a result, I have carpal tunnel and an entrapped nerve in the elbow of my left arm.

I'm left handed.

My doctor said I should stay off the computer for "a few months".

I make a living in Digital Media.
Talk about a mine sent to deter. But, guess what?

Thanks to the beauty of software, I can speak words directly into my computer.

And I still have full use of my right hand.

The process of seeing this book to fruition isn't even about me.

Because I finally finished the manuscript last night.

It's about someone reading this who has been sent a mine to deter them from completing what God has started in them.

And another mine.

And another mine.

Will you allow enemy mines to deter you?

Or will you be determined to finish the good work that God began in you?

You are not reading this by accident.

This message is intended for you or someone you know.

That's accidentally on purpose.

And that is how determined God is to help you live out your purpose, no matter how many enemy mines you encounter.

BARGAINS

Dear God: Teach us how to bargain in a way that promotes obedience that we may not bar any gains you intend for us.

If you think you are the first person to ever bargain with God, think again.

When people read Genesis 19, the focus is usually on Lot's wife.

Let's take a closer look at that chapter.

Lot was the nephew of Abraham, who was living in Sodom.

When God told Abraham about his plan to destroy Sodom and Gomorrah, he pled with God.

Abraham began bargaining with the goal of saving Lot's family.

God in his grace, accepted the bargain - ten righteous men and the cities would be saved.

But, there weren't ten.

Yet, God agreed to save Abraham's family.

So, He dispatched angels to warn Abraham's nephew.

When the angels arrived, they wanted to sleep in the street.
Lot wanted them to sleep in his home.

Bargaining.

The angels let him have his way.

Later that night when men from the town wanted to have relations with the angels, what did Lot do?

He bargained.

And offered his daughters in exchange.

The next morning, the angels pushed Lot to get going.

He hesitated.

The angels finally grabbed Lot by the arm, along with his wife and daughters.

Why?

Because even though Lot dragged his feet, God said he and his family would live.

And after being pushed and pulled by angels, Lot still hesitated.

Why?

Because he didn't want to go where God told him to go.

So he started bargaining with the angels.

Again.

He didn't want to go to the mountains.

And again, God let him have his way.

As fire rained down and lava poured upon Sodom and Gomorrah, Lot's wife looked back.

We all know what happened to her.

But, what happened to Lot? Where did all of his bargaining get him?

He was too afraid to stay in the town he bargained with God to save.

He ended up going to the mountains. Exactly where God told him to go.

And his daughters?

Perhaps they remembered the bargain he tried to make with the men of Sodom and Gomorrah.

You know, to offer his daughters up to them.

As if that was necessary.

Like he was doing the angels a favor and they needed his protection.

So, he went to live with his daughters. And they didn't bargain.

They plastered him with wine.

And then they took advantage of him.

The same way he had bargained for them to be taken advantage of.

What are we bargaining for?

As in the case of Lot, bargaining with God is often a sign of reluctance to be obedient to his plan for us.

When Abraham bargained, he did it in such a way that he received some gain.

His family was safe.

Lot's bargaining resulted in barring him from God's best for him.

Bar or Gain.

It's your choice.

But, just as with Lot, there are times that God will let you have your way.

Is that what you want?

REWARDS

Dear God: As we pray, teach us to recognize your voice so that we may receive your answer, not being bewildered or confused by it.

A tremendous example of prayer is found in the first few chapters of 1 Samuel.

Hannah was a sister wife and barren.

In the times of Israel it was believed that God closed the womb of those without children.

Married to Elkanah, his other wife Peninnah bore children and constantly derided Hannah.

But Hannah was deeply loved by her husband.

Despite being cruelly taunted, Hannah went yearly to offer a sacrifice to God.

Year after year.

Have you ever prayed for something year after year?

Once, Hannah was so upset she was reduced to tears and had no appetite.
Have you ever been that distressed?

Her husband tried to console her and assure her of his love. She pulled herself together and then quietly went to pray.

Again.

What was different about this prayer?

She had been praying year after year but this time her prayer was comprised of three elements.

1) She was "crushed in soul".
2) "She prayed to God and cried and cried – inconsolably."
3) "She made a vow."

Read the entire prayer in 1 Samuel 1:9-11.

Hannah was praying for the birth of a son, what are we praying to give birth to?

What is that thing deep in our belly that we want more than anything else?

What makes us "crushed in soul" and has caused us to cry and cry "inconsolably"?

If we want something that badly and it has not manifested year after year in prayer, could it be that we are missing the third component?

Perhaps God wants a vow from us.

Not a regular vow.

A sacrifice.

While the Bible says that obedience is better than a sacrifice, it does not negate our need to make any.

Hannah was specific in her request. She asked God to:

1) "Take a good, hard look" at her pain.
2) "Quit neglecting" her and
3) "Go into action".

Read the entire prayer in 1 Samuel 1:9-11.

She then promised she would sacrifice her son.

She wanted a son so bad, that she was willing to send him off to the temple at a young age and commit him to a life of service.

Do you want something so bad that you would give it back to God once he gave it to you?

Not most people would. With what result?

First, let's consider what happened immediately after Hannah prayed.

As she prayed, the priest thought she was drunk.

Has someone thought your prayer request was crazy? What was your response?

What did Hannah say?

Her reply can be found in 1 Samuel 1:15-16:

"I haven't been drinking. Not a drop of wine or beer. The only thing I've been pouring out is my heart."

Notice that Hannah didn't even tell the man of God what she was praying for.

Instead, she told him that she was "desperately unhappy."

She then she asked him to pray for her.

People don't need to know the specifics of your pain to pray for you.
And after pouring her heart out to God, did she sulk and cry?
Nope.

"Then she ate heartily, her face radiant."

As further proof that she gave it to God, according to 1 Samuel 1:19 – she "got up with her husband before dawn and worshipped God."

Then something miraculous happened.

"Elkanah slept with Hannah…and God began making the necessary arrangements in response to what she had asked".

Many times we pray and before we see instant results, God is making the necessary arrangements in response to what we ask!

How many times are we willing to be "up before dawn" worshipping God?

In the privacy of our home, absent of Pastor and church, do we?

When it was time for Hannah to deliver on her vow to commit Samuel to God, she didn't hesitate.

And she went to the same priest who thought she was drunk and said: (I am paraphrasing):

"You thought I was drunk, but God gave me what I asked for and now – I am dedicating my son to God to live with you".

And when Hannah prayed again, she glorified God in her joy declaring "God puts poor people on their feet again".

Are you feeling poor in spirit?

Are you inconsolable over a broken dream? Do you want to be pregnant with possibilities?

Pray.

After God gave Hannah what she wanted: one son, she honored her vow.

And then God rewarded her: three more sons and two daughters!

Identify the fire in your belly.

Cry out to God.

Commit to him.

Some prayers are intended to be between you and God.

Let people think you are crazy. They don't matter. Be willing to sacrifice.

You may be the only thing stopping God's preparation to fulfill your request.

VISION

Dear God: Please remove any debris and blinders so that we may focus clearly on your vision for us and invigorate our purpose.

Do you remember the first time you realized your gifts and talents?

Can you recall the moment you realized that you were created to be great at something?

I was in the 1st grade and we had library day at school.

My mom had taught me to read before I started attending school. I chose my first book "Where The Wild Things Are".

Then I chose another. And then another. And another.

I had so many books that I could barely carry them to the librarian's desk.

I remember the quiet laughter as I struggled and then finally pushed all twelve books onto the counter.

Then came the heartbreaking words.

"You can only take out one book at a time." As my lips quivered, I whispered:

"One book? Then why are there so many here?"

I began to sob, thinking I would never have the chance to read any of those books, and the librarian said something that stuck with me.

"Why don't you start with one? Read it and then come back and tell me what you liked about it.

Then you can take another one home."

Of course, I stayed up way past my bedtime with only the streetlight and the moon to serve as illumination.

Did I know I would be a writer?

Nope.

But in the 1st grade, I knew I could not live without having a book, composed of words in my life.

How many dreams have you tried to take out at one time?
God has a life full of amazing things planned for you.

But some visions require assignments that need to be completed one at a time.

Have you ever seen a young child with toys strewn all over the floor?

They are not thinking about the potential for danger to themselves or others.

No matter how many they are surrounded with, they can only play with one at a time.

I imagine that's how we appear to God when we have so many plans for ourselves that we aren't able to execute fully on one of them.

What roadblocks to success have we created by trying to take out too many books or playing with too many toys at one time?

Focus. God knows the plans he has for us.

If we sit quietly focused on one thing at a time he will reveal his plans for us so that we can accomplish them.

One at a time.

HANGERS

Dear God: Speak to our hearts about the quality and quantity of people in our lives.

When we contemplate our "circle of trust", we should reflect on Jesus' inner circle.

Is there a Judas hanging out in our lives?

Consider some facts about Judas taken from Matthew 9:38 – 10:4.

He was an answer to prayer.

He was called by God to be one of the Twelve.

He was given the power to cast out demons and heal the sick. Yet, he betrayed Christ.

Judas was entrusted with something valuable – money.

And it was his lust for money that caused him to betray our Lord and Savior.

Who is holding your money?

And by money I don't mean finances.
Who have you entrusted with the secrets of your dreams, which spell out your future?

Who is trying to bury you, ready to sell you out to the highest bidder?

If anyone in your circle has a Judas spirit of deception, greed, or lust for money why have you permitted him or her to stay?

Jesus did it in order that scripture might be fulfilled.

What's your reasoning?

Surround yourself with those who have no hidden agenda, no ulterior motives and who don't lust after money, power or greed.

Don't fall victim by allowing those who pray with you to prey upon you.

The Judas spirit may manifest itself under the guise of "doing the Lord's work".

God will allow people to enter our lives to teach us a lesson. How long will it take for us to learn from it?

One characteristic of the Judas spirit is being remorseful of the consequences, not the sin.

When Jesus mentioned a betrayal, Judas responded with a simple question:

"It isn't me, is it?" Matthew 26:25

The Judas spirit is often in a state of constant denial.

When he became remorseful, it was too late. Why?

Because he sold Jesus out to people who had their own hidden agendas. Matthew 27:3,4

Watch out for the Judas spirit in your life.

Because if you don't, just as with Judas, God will allow you to hang yourself.

TOOLS

Dear God: Thanks for the reminder that our value is intended to increase, our worth should always be priceless and you delight in our growth.

Many of you reading this have various dreams and goals.

But, do you know what you are working with?

A successful carpenter has all of the appropriate tools at his disposal.

More importantly, he knows which tool to use to get the job done in an efficient manner.

Not only is he aware of what is in his toolbox, but he also knows when to use each tool.

I was recently reminded by angels in my life that I already have what I need to succeed and so do you!

Our gifts and talents are tools to be used to fulfill the dreams God placed in our heart.

A wise person continually seeks ways to grow and expand.

It's not always easy, but faith requires a leap, not a step.

Look at your network and appreciate the value of reciprocity.

Reaping and sowing is not merely a one for one exchange.

What have you invested in the growth of another?

When we plant seeds, we expect a harvest – not a mere seed in return.

Exponentially.

Apple seeds blossom into trees bearing fruit that feed many people.

Year after year after year.

My challenge to you:

Take some time to re-examine your gifts and talents minus your hopes and dreams.

Take some time to introspectively look at the value proposition you offer.

If you think you have nothing to offer, think again.

You have a toolkit at your disposal.

God created you with gifts and talents that only you can develop.

What's in your toolkit?

If you don't know where your value lies, ask three trusted friends or colleagues to list 5 of your strengths.

I intentionally omitted family because often love overshadows truth.

Look at American Idol hopefuls.

Many people have dreams dashed because no one was honest about their gifts.

Sometimes we need others to show us the value of what we are working with.

Often others see value in things we take for granted.

Therein lies the key to unlocking your gifts and talents.

Those most gifted by God are often blocked from full expression merely because they don't accept how amazing their gift is.

Which simply means they don't appreciate the value of the tools in their kit.

Don't succumb to fear. Let go of every excuse.

We already have what we need.

Examine your gifts and then take that huge leap of faith to fulfill your dreams.

I am.

APART

Dear God: Thank you for being my Jehovah-Jireh, Jehovah-Rophe, Jehovah-Nissi, Jehovah-Shalom - even when I feel apart from you.

Why is it that when trouble, doubt, worry, fear or insecurity knocks, we hesitate to answer it with a prayer or promise of God?

Our God is more powerful, stronger and greater than anything in the world.

Not just the planet, earth, continent, state, or city.

Yet, when we are feeling down, or less than blessed, we try to figure out a solution apart from God.

Often, we try to make a solution on our own.

And when it doesn't work out, we resort to prayer.

"Well all there is left to do is pray and hope that God answers."

Prayer should be our first resort, not the last.

We should invite God to become a part of our solution. Not apart from the solution.

If we truly believe God is all-powerful and loves us enough to know the hairs on our head, why do we hesitate to pray?

More often than not, it's because we are not comfortable with something that we have done contrary to his will.

When the prophet Nathan confronted David about his sin, God wanted confession.

God knew all of the gory details as it went down!

In fact, he knew that David was lusting after another man's wife in his heart!

God knew that David wanted Bathsheba so bad that he was willing to kill for her.

And when it was done - God wanted David to admit it to him.

When Nathan presented David's sin to him as if it were someone else's, David's "morals" kicked in.

But, it wasn't until God exposed David through Nathan that his conscience kicked in.

And yet, God forgave him.

There were consequences to his sin, yet David is most remembered as being a man after God's own heart.

God did it for David he will do it for you.

Stop trying to find a way out of the darkness, because you refuse to get on your knees and clear your heart before the one who has a way out!

I have lived in condemnation and shame - that was such a tremendous burden.

It took years for me to view myself as someone God could love.

Free yourself so that prayer becomes your first resort.

Not your fall back plan.

Realize that your shortcomings and weaknesses do not confine you.

Don't let them confine you.

Permit your experiences to refine you.

Accept the gifts of God's mercy, love, grace and Jesus' life.

You are precious in the eyes of God.

Condemnation, guilt and shame are tricks of the enemy to keep you apart from God.

The truth is: God wants to be a part of your life.

Don't let anything keep you from God's love.

He won't allow anything or anyone to keep you apart from him.

Nothing.

GUTS

Dear God: Thank you for wisdom, confirmation and the ability and willingness to heed the groaning of the spirit.

You've got a gut and it's far more useful than serving as a bottomless pit to indulge food fantasies.

How many times have you said or heard "I knew that was going to happen!"

Some people refer to that feeling as a premonition.

I prefer to refer to it as your gut.

God's Undisputed Truth at work in your life.

"Don't trust her – it will not go well with her and she only intends evil towards you."

"I know your heart wants him, but he isn't yours."

"Get your heart right and wait for the man I am sending you."

"Why are you sharing your dream with the very one who is plotting to turn it into a nightmare?"

When we go against that gut feeling, consider the consequences of denying God's Undisputed Truth.

When we are walking with God – he is our Gut.

Someone reading this needs to hear clearly: God is trying to tell you something.

Stop saying "I had a feeling!"

It's your gut.

God's Undisputed Truth.

Act on the feeling!

How many blessings have we delayed by not going with the gut?

Spend some time alone with God.

You will be amazed!

DISCOURAGEMENT

Dear God: Speak to discouraged hearts and massage them tenderly, pumping them full of courage.

What is it that causes us to lose perspective and see our dreams as a nightmare or unattainable?

Let's examine a few reasons discouragement can take over and destroy our ambition.

Jealousy: Insecurity stemming from the realization that we are not all that we can be as we watch others succeed.

Insecurity: Feeling that we are not adequate enough, fed by a lack of trust in what God has gifted us to do.

Pride: Foolishly forgetting that God gave us our talents and without him they cannot be perfected.

Associations: Someone not worthy of our trust has our ear and is slowly feeding us venom, poisoning our hearts and minds.

Steer clear of jealousy, insecurity and pride.

Be wise in your associations.

These things will permeate your spirit and cause grief to your soul.

Determine to make today the last of the worst, cursed and the first of the best, blessed days of your life.

Only you can decide if you will drown in a pool of discouragement or wade in a sea of encouragement.

Will you be brave enough to choose encouragement over discouragement?

Courage.

It really is your choice.

SHARDS

Dear God: Continue to guide our introspective process thereby rejecting denial and the damage it brings to our ego and perspective.

Sometimes we need to remove a veil, peel through layers and examine our roots in order to see clearly.

As our parents raise us, some of the deeply ingrained lessons we learn are associated with their own scarred soul.

And we don't even know it.

As a young girl, my mom taught me to be a victim and to fear men.

The same woman birthed in me a remarkably strong love for God and his Word.

While I was openly taught the Word of God by speech, I was covertly receiving impressionable messages through her behavior.

In my gut, I knew something wasn't right but I did not know how to change what I felt, let alone recognize it to be able to express it.

Now that I am on the other side as a mother who has made the choice to change generational behaviors, one behavior stays in my head.

My stepfather was physically abusive.

We saw it; we heard it and my brother and I finally took a stand against it at 13 and 14 years old.

One day, I heard them screaming and yelling and I got a knife.

As my mom screamed from being hit, my brother grabbed him and I simply said:

"If you hit my mother again, I will kill you."

And I meant it.

My mother stayed with him until her death and although the incident was never discussed, I never saw him hit her or yell at her again.

Through God's grace, they both became different people.

Yet, whether they knew it or not, that situation told my spirit "you need to fight so this never, ever happens to you".

But, it did.

It wasn't until I was an adult with children of my own that I realized the messages my soul received growing up.

My mom chose a man who would fight for her and protect her, something she never had when being repeatedly sexually assaulted as a child.

But she never factored in that his anger could be directed towards her as well with the same results.

Neither did I.

Take some time finding out whom you are. Study your DNA.

Learn what has been deposited into your soul.

Examine the shards you were exposed to in your childhood.

Some of us are walking around with shards of broken glass embedded in our soul by other wounded souls.

As we extract those shards of glass from our lives, it will hurt and we will bleed.

But there will be healing.

The first step for some may be to forgive the person who cut you with the glass.

Realize they learned to hurt and taught you to feel pain due to shards in their life.

It won't be easy but it must be done.

Trade in that pain.

You can reverse the cycle.

Let's take out the glass.

Heal your soul and break the cycle.

MIRRORS

Dear God: Speak to our hearts, whisper words of discernment in our ears and infuse our spirits with power.

How is your heart health?

"Out of the heart's abundance the mouth speaks."

What is your heart saying?

We often associate our heart with emotions, particularly those of love and hate.

But the heart is the core of all things we speak.

Since our words hold tremendous power, we need to check our heart.

The heart is home to our deepest desires, unspoken thoughts and secrets beyond measure.

It may be evidenced in what we say, how we say it or when and where we say it, but our heart will eventually manifest in our speech.

What have you been talking about?

Is it in line with your deepest desires?
Have you found yourself saying things that you regret?

Do you feel your speech has misrepresented you?

Are you suddenly aware that you have spoken powerful words that negatively impact your future?

Check your heart.

Just as God hardened and softened Pharaoh's heart, he can remold yours as well.

When your heart has become hardened to the point of ungratefulness, ask God to send you a mirror.

When you feel like you haven't made any progress, and your heart is constantly sighing, ask God to send you a mirror.

A mirror is someone that is a reflection of a major life obstacle that you have overcome.

Ask for the mirror to help your heart.

To see someone who is currently going through something that God delivered you from has the potential to improve your heart health.

What can a mirror do?

1). Usher a spirit of unparalleled gratefulness into your heart when you realize the reflection of how far you've come.

2). Instill hope as you help mold another heart by transparently sharing your testimony and sharing how they can do it as well.

3). Provide a chance for you to have heartfelt moments of rejoicing, extolling God's grace.

Check your heart to improve what you say.

Words have power. Your heart holds the key; ask for a mirror to unlock it.

Clear the clutter from your heart so that the abundance of words, which flow, will result in a legacy of blessings.

And one day, when you look in the mirror, the reflection of you will be enough to remind of you how to help your heart.

CHANGE

Dear God: Teach us the value of change. Show us how to make daily deposits towards the success you have planned for us.

My mom kept a change purse when I was younger. It was full of pennies, nickels, dimes and quarters.

The small purse would get so heavy that she would then need to transfer the contents to a larger container.

Once that container became full, we would all sit together and put the coins in paper wrappers.

She would then take the carefully wrapped coins to the bank and deposit the money into a savings account.

In thinking about making changes in our daily lives, I suppose that would be a great model to follow.

Each day, collect small amounts of change – take small steps to do something new, something positive, and something good.

It doesn't matter if the change we make is small as in a penny.

Some days we may make significant quarter or even half-dollar sized changes.

Change is change and all change is valuable.

Eventually our "change" purse will become so full that we will have planted enough seeds to deposit, much like sowing seed.

Imagine what our "account" will look like over time when we reap the harvest from our deposits!

The difference between the person in the mirror and the person you want to be is change.

The comfort of the familiar can keep you from going to another level. Growth requires change.

Many have entered a crossroads in life and instead of forging straight ahead they reached back longingly into the familiar.

Often in the process of opening and walking through new doors the most difficult part is leaving the familiar.

Step away from the familiar.

It doesn't happen over night and won't be instantaneous, but the culmination of all you have accomplished is destined to open new doors.

DISCIPLINE

Dear God: Thank you for showing me the way out of temptation and into the blessing of singleness.

Abstinence. Celibacy. Single. Married. Divorced.

They are all words.

More importantly, they are all choices.

And more often than not, they are related to that three-letter word that so many people have trouble discussing.

Sex.

I did not wake up one morning and decide "I'm not going to have sex for more than years".

I did not suddenly decide, I think I am going to stop dating for a while.

I did wake up one morning after having sex with someone I wasn't married to yet madly in love with and cry my eyes out.

It wasn't the first time.

He never noticed my silent tears.

The agony of immeasurable pleasure combined with unbearable guilt.

But my soul was tired.

I wasn't mad at men.

I was tired of enjoying the best sex ever and immediately feeling disconnected from the one I love the most: God.

I was tired of starting my prayers with "God, I'm sorry, I did it again and it's really hard for me to stay away because I love him."

I was tired of not feeling free to take my problems to God because I knew I was intentionally sinning.

I was tired of trying to ignore God whispering in my ear as I got myself all dressed up and smelling good for my booty call.

And most importantly, I was tired of not enjoying the full benefits of living a life completely lived for God.

It wasn't random sex.

It was someone I loved more than I had ever loved before.

I was monogamous.

But, I ended the relationship.

When it was over, I was sad. I even tried to go back.

And I couldn't understand how I could hurt so much.

I couldn't understand why I could feel so convicted for doing something that felt so good, so spiritual.

But, I knew: I needed to obey God.

What was I to do? Go find another man to sleep with?

Nope. It would not have been the same.

I realized that each time I gave my body to a man; I was taking something away from God.

I was also depriving myself.

Depriving myself of a clean conscience.

It didn't matter what others around me did. I knew what God told me!

After that, when a man approached me, I turned him down. I needed to learn the art of discipline.

I had spent so many years of my life, using my body for my own pleasure that I knew I needed to do some soul cleansing.

So I took it one day at a time.

One guy at a time.

One No at a time.

And now, I have not only days of celibacy, I have years of celibacy.

Discipline.

Do I miss a relationship? Yup!

Do I desire companionship? Yup.

But, this time, I'm waiting on God.

Are there times I want sex? Um, heck yeah!

I know what I need and want in a relationship and I won't settle anymore.
And as I learned discipline, guess what happened?

I made a lot of amazing friends.

I found my purpose.

I honed my talents.

I focused.

I created an online radio show.

I pursued my writing career.

I began a successful television career.

I started my own business.

I learned so much about myself.

And I got closer to God than I ever imagined possible.

I hear him more clearly.

The nights of staining my pillow with tears of guilt and shame are long gone.

I know people like to say, "just give it to God".

The truth is: It doesn't happen in an instant.

It's a daily decision.

So, if people ridicule you for being celibate, ignore the ignorance.

The orgasm they enjoy for a moment can't compete with God's everlasting love!

Even in my walk towards the celibate life, I slipped up a few times.

I once went a month, then three months and finally I learned to stop counting how long it's been since I've "had some".

I started counting how long my body has belonged to God!

And now, I'm eagerly anticipating that man, my future husband that God has in store just for me.

Because I am disciplined.

Does that make me perfect?

Nope.

Does it mean that I am any better than those who are not celibate?

Nope.

It simply means that in this area of my life, I have made a decision to be obedient.

And obedience is better than a sacrifice.

HELP

Dear God: Please align our hearts, motives and definitions to match yours as you order our steps forward in purpose.

You cannot help someone who refuses to be helped, no more than you can make someone love you.

For every person that you want to help, there's another who wants to be helped.

Stop wasting your energy on those who may deserve help, but, refuse to accept it.

Just because they are not ready, doesn't mean we should love them any less.

Some people's level of self-esteem is so low that they consider themselves unworthy of help.

Continue to love them but divert your good will efforts to someone who accepts that they are worthy of your help.

If a person needs help and doesn't accept it, maybe you are not the person to help them.

Keep it moving.

In some instances, our definition of help differs greatly from the person seeking assistance.

Many people are looking for a "hook-up" or define help as doing everything for them, instead of working with them.

On the other hand, some people have too much pride in accepting help.

It makes no sense to pray to God for help and not accept his provision just because you don't like the vessel or messenger he sent.

When I needed help, I rarely asked and when I did, I was devastated when no one would help.

I had to learn to rely on God to use people to help me.

I had to give myself permission to ask and receive.

The sad truth is that often the people whom we perceive as being able to help us the most, may be unwilling to help.

Conversely those whom we want help from the most are often ill equipped to do so.

What if we relied solely on God to make the decision of whom to send to help us and in which form the help should come?

God's word says we have not, because we ask not. It really is that simple.

God says he will meet our daily needs. He didn't say he would dump a million dollars in the bank.

If God chose to provide you with a lifetime supply of food, would you turn it down?

If he showed you how to make a million dollars, would you be willing to put in the work to do it?

How do you define help?

If you give it some thought, you may already have all of the help you need.

No

Dear God: Thank you for the gift of no and the reminder that we all have the power to choose.

What could you accomplish if you said no more readily to some things?

From childhood, our emotions have been trained to fear receiving a no in response to a request.

Our heart shrinks upon rejection.

Likewise, often we carry a burden and are often reluctant to say no, even when we desire to most.

But, what if we are limiting ourselves by refusing to say no to some things in our lives?

Words are powerful, yet perception and perspective can aid in unlocking keys to their potential.

For example:

What if our no became a catalyst for more?

What if we said no to things that sound good short term, but are diminished over time?

What if no simply means I won't do or accept something because it is not sufficient.

What if we looked at no as meaning I want Not Only this, but also more?

How many of us are willing to say no now to things that will free us up to be ready for the yes?

Have you ever been filled will regret after saying yes simply because you lacked patience and sought instant gratification?

Learn to appreciate your right to choose.

Sometimes saying no is the most freeing thing you can do in preparation for great yes moments.

What will you say no to today so that you are Not Only ready for a yes, but also free to receive more when it comes along?

RESET

Dear God: Keep us focused on what lies ahead, leaving the past behind, yet using discernment when looking to the left and right.

Each day that we awaken, we have a chance to start fresh.

A fresh start does not mean acting as if yesterday never happened, while repeating prior mistakes.

A fresh start does means remembering what happened yesterday, looking at it with fresh eyes and working towards the good.

A fresh start also means being accountable and responsible for our actions.

Within the biblical principle of reaping and sowing, we have the ability to sow different seed, to achieve better results.

Perhaps you have harvested some bad crop.

Maybe in this season of harvest much of your fruit is rotten or spoiled.

Start now to scrap the bad crop.

Find better soil and plant good seeds for a better harvest.

How? Pay attention to where you sow seed.

What is important to you? What feeds you? What drives you?

Examine your motives and methods.

What influences you most?

Who speaks authoritatively into your life?

What is the first thing you do when you awaken?

Are you waking up asking others to pray for you, yet neglecting to pray for yourself?

Are you so wrapped up in meeting the needs of others that you are not planting seeds into your own life?

What is the process of your life saying about where, how, what and when you sow?

All seeds do not grow in every season.

Are you allowing weeds of jealousy, discontent, depression, and enmity to choke up your plants as they start growing?

Let's decide now to stop complaining about what we are harvesting and start sowing better crop for a richer harvest!

Surround yourself with people who nourish and enrich your life.

Remove those who threaten to snuff out your very existence.

No matter the source of the weeds - remove them from your life.

Don't be left wringing your hands wondering how you lost it all!

Make today and every day that you have the breath of life a new opportunity to hit the reset button.

FAILURE

Dear God: Thank you for continuing to hold our hands each time we fall down, guiding us to reach higher heights.

As an infant learning to walk, we fall. Several times.

No one has ever had a fall so bad that it caused him or her to fear learning to walk.

The desire to walk is so strong that babies will get up over and over again.

No matter how many times they fall. No matter how much it hurts. Why?

Because there is always someone cheering them on.

From the moment a baby is born, people marvel at their smiles.

Parents brag about their first word as if no one ever spoke it before. And parents wait with bated breath for that first step.

The milestone of a child's first unaided step elicits joy, laughter and happiness from both parent and child.

No child's development is ever measured in terms of how many times they fell before they started walking.

But, as we develop into adults something changes. We associate falling with failure.

We don't always have people cheering on our successes.

We don't always have a person to hold our hand or soothe us when we fall.

We have God.

He doesn't look at our falls as failures. I believe he sees them as fell-ures.

He's not counting how many times we've fallen.

He's fully vested in the end result.

He wants us to win.

What if we started today, to go back to infancy?

What if we started today to look at each fall as getting us one step closer to walking?

Unsupported. And on our own.

God has our back, long before we can see what's in front of us.

Expect to fall. Refuse to stay down.

Don't be afraid to get up and walk again.

You might not see it, but I am here.

Always cheering you on.

And so is God.

RELATIONSHIPS

Dear God: Thank you for the gift of reflection and analysis, which deter deception and paralysis.

Check the status of your relationship with everyone in your life.

When society asks our relationship status, they are solely interested in our romantic life.

What about our other relationships?

How is our relationship with our siblings?

How well do we relate to our parents?

Who are the people we allow to speak into our lives and life or death to our dreams?

While our relationship with God is paramount, we cannot neglect our relationships with others.

Today, I want to share something with you that will greatly improve your life and your relationship status: An MBA!

I'm not talking about a degree. But, I am speaking of something that requires effort, study and testing.

MBA = Mutual Benefit Associations!

When people think of mutual benefit, they seek out what will benefit them and how they can benefit others simultaneously.

What if we approached each relationship from the perspective of expecting to positively impact another person?

Take some time today and evaluate your relationships from the perspective of them being a Mutual Benefit Association.

Why?

It's simple math: Anyone or any thing that takes away from you without adding value is a liability!

God's law is reaping and sowing.

Everything we do produces something.

There are times when some relationships need to be put on hold.

Some are worthy of more time, nurturing and development.

Others simply need to be ended.

Examine the value of your relationships. It's very much worth the effort.

The more we strive to be intentional about our associations, the closer to greatness we become.

Sometimes in order for God to enlarge your territory, you need to tighten your circle.

Never forget that saying no to one relationship may be necessary to open the door to your next opportunity.

Resolve

Dear God: I refuse to speak any re-solutions over my life. You are first and only solution to everything in my life.

Many of us feel pressure to adopt New Year's Resolutions.

For some it's a tradition.

For others it comes as a result of reflections about the previous year.

I gave up New Year re-solutions when I accepted that God is the only, permanent solution.

Why try to re-solve what he's taken care of?

How many times have you made a New Year's resolution?

Re-solutions are just putting a band-aid on what you never fixed the year before.

The reason people don't stick to re-solutions is because they have what they need to change year round and still don't do it.

Too often, people are unfocused and become discouraged when they can measure from year to year with no results.

You don't have to wait until one year ends before you evaluate every area of your life.

What will you do today that will impact tomorrow?

What decision can you make now to bolster your chances for success in the future?

I want to encourage you to ponder five questions today, to set you on the path to success:

1) Who have you walked with this year, that you need to run from now to experience breakthrough?

2) Who have you walked away from erroneously and need to run back to in order to experience breakthrough?

3) What have you done to block your own blessings and need to stop in order to experience breakthrough?

4) What things have you not done in the spirit of procrastination or self-sabotage and need to get done to experience breakthrough?

5) Who are you allowing to check your moral compass? Is God the standard for greatness in your life?

By answering those five questions honestly, with a view to being all that God has created you to be, you are moving towards greatness!

At any given moment, we can choose. We decide.

And we need to continue to choose on a daily basis.

After all, we already have solutions to everything in our lives. And what we can't handle - God's got us covered.

Stop re-solving.

Get it right the first time - choose.

NOTHING

Dear God: Thank you for revelation that provides clarity in the simplest of ways.

I read a simple sentence one morning that blew me away.

"Why do you sit around here and look at one another?"

Seems simple and I've read it more times than I can count.

The phrase is found in Genesis 42:1.

And it was not the words themselves, but the bigger picture of the story around them.

Most of us know the story of Joseph and how his brothers figuratively and literally hated him upon.

But, when we look at the context of those words "Why do you sit around here and look at one another?" it explains a lot.

At the times the words were uttered, there was a famine.

Why didn't Joseph's adult brothers who had families and were caring for their aging father go out to look for food?

The fact that their ailing father had to tell them to go get food for their families speaks volumes.

"Why do you sit around here and look at one another?"

Those people who are downplaying your gifts are doing what Joseph's brothers did: sitting around looking, doing nothing!

When people discount your dreams, as Joseph's brothers did - realize the reason.

They are sitting around looking at you, while doing nothing.

No matter how many people are against you, know that just as God promoted Joseph - he has a promotion for you!

Even if your "brothers" sell you out - God will set things straight.

Whatever you do, make sure that you are not surrounded by people who "sit around and look at one another."

And more importantly, make sure you are not sitting on your hands neglecting God's gifts within you.

ALONE

Dear God: Thank you for the model of Christ, who recognized the need of breaking away into alone time.

Often we live our lives constantly performing on the stage of work, friendships, relationships and family.

Perhaps is causes us to shy away from just BEING.

Not everyone is comfortable in his or her own skin.

That is a growth process. But how will you even know what skin you are in if you don't get to know yourself?

It took a while for me to appreciate the value of my company.

I developed those things I liked and demolished those I didn't.

I learned that I did not have to accept every invitation to go out or answer the phone every time it rang.

I learned that not every question that demands a response deserves an answer.

I learned that I can CHOOSE whom I want to give the power to speak over and into my life.

I learned that I am not obligated to contribute to anyone's happiness, nor limit mine because of another's.

I learned that just as God has blessings for me with my name on them, there are others he won't release to me until I release some things.

I no longer live under the faux obligation of loyalty, which believes you should never evict people from your life.

I learned that sometimes God says no to protect us, while preparing us for the Next Opportunity.

The Bible tells of Jesus slipping away from the crowd on several occasions to be alone.

Do we ever allow ourselves alone time?

God spoke to Adam in the "breezy part of the day".

Set some time aside to be alone with yourself and with God.

You will learn amazing things about yourself and have a new appreciation of just how wonderfully you are made.

EXPECTING

Dear God: Please manage our expectations and let us know when to let go in order that we may grow.

A lot of times we expect things to go a certain way. Not just in relationships but in life in general.

We expect that if we do a great job, we will be rewarded.

We expect that if we pour our hearts into our work, we will see results.

We expect that our gifts and talents will take us to higher heights.

And, often, we expect that our lives are going according to plan.

But, according to whose plan?

At some point in our lives, we decide what we want to be, what we want to do.

I'm not talking about business plans or five year plans.

I mean the things that are buried deep in our heart.

And sometimes, we take a chance.

We take what we like to refer to as a leap of faith.

We do that, because, we believe with all of our heart that this is what we are supposed to do.

When things are not progressing as we had hoped or when things get tougher than we expected, we need to make a decision.

Will I stay with this plan or will I go?

It's more troubling for creatives, because they feel like they've been pregnant with the expectation of birth for so long.

Unfortunately, some people will have labor pains and get excited and prepared for the delivery, only to see the dream was stillborn.

Sometimes, it's time to move on.

It doesn't mean that you didn't nurture the dream enough.

And it most definitely, does not mean that it's time for you to insert someone else into your dream.

What God has for you, is for you.

Nothing can stop it.

It may be time to something go so you can free yourself to receive the seed for the dream that you were meant to birth.

And the dream you were meant to birth is intended for you to raise and develop through maturity.

Whoever this message is intended for, whomever this resonates with, already knows that it's time to say goodbye to some things.

Stop blaming every failure or setback on an attack of the enemy.

God can never fail, so if you believe in your plan more than God does, what can you expect the results to be?

Let's start to look at letting go as letting grow.

By adding the letters R and W to the word go, we can start to view some things in the Right Way.

Clear the clutter.

Prepare a space for you to grow.

When a child is lost through miscarriage, often a woman needs a procedure referred to as a D&C.

The purpose of the procedure is to ensure that any debris is removed and the womb is thoroughly clean.

Now's the time to clean your womb.

Remove the debris - prepare to receive a new implantation.

And prepare to expect again.

JOY

Dear God: Thank you for constantly refining me while defining the motives of others, protecting my joy.

Have you ever felt like you want to hide out in a cave and not hear the voice of anyone?

Have you ever wished you had a time machine so you could fast forward to the NEXT season in your life?

Living your best life is not always easy.

Anyone who says so is either delusional or a liar.

We don't live our lives in a silo, sectioned off from other people and events.

Our day of total bliss could come crashing down at any second - because of the thoughts, speech or actions of another person.

What matters most on a day-to-day basis is two-fold:

1). How we react to situations and
2) How our actions affect others.

Instead of focusing on how others have "ruined" our day, let's regroup and consider how our actions will affect another today.

Taking a few minutes to think before we speak/act, will make a difference in the level of joy in our lives.

Especially when it seems like the hardest thing to do.

Continue to examine the motives/actions of people around you, there's no shortage of knives floating around.

Don't allow the actions of one person to negatively impact the way you treat others, don't give them that much power.

Learn how to create boundaries in your life that will continue to exist whether others respect them or not.

Guard your heart and thoughts.

Pay attention to those who whisper and gossip about others.

They are doing the same about you in your absence.

People can only stab you in the back when you let your guard down.

Surround yourself with people who walk alongside of you, not behind you.

Stop feeling honored when people say they want to be like you.

They want your glory, not your story.

Don't allow any person or event to rob you of your joy.

They aren't worthy.

Remind yourself constantly of your accomplishments and goals - remove yourself from the company of bottom feeders.

Continue to tighten your circle as God enlarges your territory.

Forgiveness is not reconciliation.

Your decision not to reconcile does not mean you are holding a grudge.

Realize that sometimes, just as you have had enough of people, they may have had enough of you.

No matter the circumstance, exit with dignity.

You have an entire day ahead of you.

Use it to give and receive joy, love and peace.

When you lay your head on your pillow at night, you will be glad you did!

HATERS

Dear God: Protect us from our thoughts and shift our hearts as you reveal your heart to us.

Haters: Those who berate or envy your success and hard work.

There are many trains of thought as to how to deal with "haters".

Some say ignore them - it means you are doing something right.

Others say haters should serve as "elevators", pushing you to work harder.

I believe there is a biblical principle applicable in every area of life.

Even "haters".

I previously subscribed to letting "haters" push me to work harder.

No more.

Now, I've made a decision based on Bible principle.

I have read Matthew 5:11,12 many times:

"Not only that—count yourselves blessed every time people put you down or throw you out or speak lies about you to discredit me.

"What it means is that the truth is too close for comfort and they are uncomfortable.

"You can be glad when that happens—give a cheer, even! —for though they don't like it, I do!

"And all heaven applauds. And know that you are in good company.

"My prophets and witnesses have always gotten into this kind of trouble."

While I previously cringed at the thought of being happy to have "haters", I now fully appreciate why I should.

The Scripture tells us to count ourselves blessed when people put us down or lie about us.

Why?

Because they open the door for God to show up.

It's about so much more than a "show of proof" that we're "doing something right".

It's more about how God will be glorified. Not about me.

As I think about "haters" and the role they have played in my life, I came to a realization:

Sometimes we invite them in.

How?

By insisting that "haters" motivate us.

Train your mind to believe that you require negativity to be inspired and you will attract it.

PROCESS

Dear God: I am confident that you will manifest the desires you placed in my heart, no matter the process.

Many of us labor over prayer and become burdened when we are eagerly waiting for God to manifest what we KNOW he has promised us.

This happens when we pray in accordance with things that God has deposited directly in our spirit and whispered in our hearts.

These are things that we have heard escape the mouths of others as our spirit recognizes each syllable uttered as confirmation.

The One, who firmly planted the seed of desire deeply within us, fertilizes it each time his whispered words echo inwardly.

Not being certain of how or when to proceed often results in doubt, disappointment, confusion and bitterness.

The answer is simple: Process.

God is a God of process as evidenced in his creation of the earth.

He was very intentional and nothing was accidental or left to chance. Creation happened in a very orderly manner.

In fact, the bible confirms that He is a God, not of disorder, but of peace. (1 Cor. 14:33)

The Apostle Paul further encourages us to do things in an orderly way. (1 Cor. 14:40)

But, how can we emulate God and have peace when we are not certain of how he plans to fulfill the very dreams he has given us?

In Genesis 37, we learn that a 17-year-old young man named Joseph had a dream that he was to be exalted above his brothers.

God did not show to Joseph how or when, yet Joseph chose to reveal the dream to his brothers.

When I was 17, I went to a movie theater with my family to see the movie "The Wiz".

During the dance scene for "Brand New Day" I started bawling openly, like a baby.

When my mom asked what was wrong, I told her that I should have "been there."

And when she asked me if I wanted to be an actress, I told her no.

I wanted to be behind the camera helping them make it because I knew they had so much fun.

I had no idea what that entailed. I had never heard of television production. I wasn't even sure how people got started.

I never gave it a second thought until years later – after God released me into what he had planted in me that day.

Just as with Joseph, my family didn't understand. I wasn't pursuing what God had planted in me, but I KNEW what I wanted to do.

However, as in the case of Joseph, it was not until many seasons later that God gave me a glimpse of what he had in store for me.

What God has planted in your spirit, will continue to take root.

It will blossom and grow as he sends people and circumstances in your life to nurture and develop your passion.

Don't ever begrudge the process.

It was not until 13 years later that God promoted Joseph to where he wanted him.

I did not enter the world of television until more than 20 years later.

Joseph's process included betrayal from his family, being wrongly imprisoned and watching God answer the prayers of others before him.

No matter where you are in your process, God will be with you, just as he was with Joseph.

Even in prison, the Bible says that God was with him and gave him success. (Genesis 39:23)

Respect the process.

God knows exactly what he's doing. His timing is always perfect.

DANGER

Dear God: Please protect me from dangers seen and unseen.

As much as I love writing, prayer is the thing that sustains me.

Prayer is the blood flowing through my veins, the pulsing of my heart, the sweetest thing I've ever known.

Prayer is the pouring out of every heartache, the mourning before the joy that comes in the morning – it is my LIFE.

If I could not pray, I would cease to exist.

Every breath I take is a testimony to the power of prayer.

It's not just that I believe in the power of prayer.

I know God hears my prayers and answers them.

They are not mere empty words, they are me pouring out my heart to the ONE who loves me more than words can express.

Prayer is the key by which the doors of communication with my Heavenly Father are opened.

Prayer is the thing that solidifies and confirms my relationship with God.

It is because of prayer that I have survived every attack of the enemy on my life.

It is because of prayer that my children are covered – even when they don't realize it.

It is because of prayer that I have a roof over my head, and food to eat.

And it is prayer that constantly saves me, over and over again.

One of my daily prayers is that God protect me from dangers seen and unseen.

He has continued to do that. More times than we know, we are in harm's way and that was the case for me on Good Friday 2011.

Good Friday is the day set aside to commemorate the death of Jesus Christ at Calvary.

That year, I was so caught up in work, I confess, that I thought of the significance of the day only briefly.

After leaving work that Friday, I had a few errands to run.

Although I had planned on taking the 7:50 pm bus, I was running late and thought the next bus would arrive at 8:30 pm.

Then I got a feeling in my gut that I needed to check the bus schedule.

I never carry a bus schedule with me and only check it online when going to work. But, I had a feeling…

To my delight and surprise there was an 8:10 pm bus.

After all, it was running on a holiday schedule.

I called my son when I got off the bus and told him he should order dinner because I was too tired to cook.

When I got to my house, I decided to go back out to the store one block away.

I stopped at home first, to give my son the money to pay for dinner and went to the store.

There was no one in the store, other than the clerk and myself. We spoke briefly and as I exited the store, I felt danger.

Although I was only 15 steps away from where I was headed, I felt the unmistakable dread of danger strongly,

I remember the words I prayed: "God, please let me make it home safely.

Protect me from danger seen and unseen.

I don't know what it is, but, please spare my life."

I looked all around and the street was like a ghost town. I saw nothing!

And once I prayed, I felt safe.

The feeling of danger passed and I was secure in knowing that God had protected me.

I realized I had forgotten to get something else from the store.

I was about to go back, but I was just too tired and decided against it.

Then it happened.

The sound that seemed so insignificant at the time. I asked my son what did it sound like to him and he replied "Probably someone banging on something."

He was wrong.

That sound was gunshots.

Fired in the store that I had just left.

In the same store that I almost decided to go back to. Two days later, the police were at my front door.

I was the last person alive in the store with that young man.

Immediately after I left, his murderers entered.

As the police questioned me, I was sickened, frightened, saddened and thankful all at once.

I knew that the same Christ, who died at Calvary and rose on the third day, spared my life on that day.

"Dear God: Please protect me from dangers seen and unseen."

I never saw a thing
.
As I reflect on that day today, I urge you to seek God in prayer.

Take some time today to think about all that he has done for you.

You are not alive by accident.

You are not reading this book by accident.

There is a reason you are alive at this very moment and reading this words at this very time.

It might not be for you. It might be for someone who you know.

Please, pray now.

Pour out your heart to God. Even if you have never done it before, just start with this:

"Dear God: Please protect me from dangers seen and unseen."

Today is not just any other day.

It is the day that I celebrate my God, who loves me so much that he hears and answers my prayers.

It is the day that I will pray to a God who gave his son's life for ours.

My God who loves me so much, that he communicates with me and lets me know when I should stop, when I should go – even when I don't know why.

It is the day that I will reflect on the life I am living, the legacy that I wish to leave.

While seeking God's forgiveness for anything in my life that does not reflect him.

This the day that I will continue to praise God, knowing that the voices of a million angels could not express my gratitude.

And I am grateful to have angels watching all over me, reading to provide protection at God's command.

I don't run from danger. I turn to God in prayer.

RAINBOWS

Dear God: I thank you for this day and the breath of life you've given me. It's my honor to serve by living an intentional in purpose life.

No matter your personal circumstances, every person reading this is blessed to awaken this morning.

In times of difficulty, it's hard to look past storms to see the beauty of the rainbow and the promise it holds.

But there are rainbows.

There is always the promise of God.

When you can't hold on to anything else, why not trust God again?

Today, be determined to discard any thing or person that drains your spirit, leaving you hopeless.

Seek out those who infuse you with encouragement, even if it means making the hard choices.

Sit under the table of people who choose God's blessed, not merely settling for their best.

Most importantly: stay connected to what you love, for that will bring you the purest form of joy coupled with peace of mind.

Life is tough.

Some relationships crumble and others are merely on hiatus. Be true to yourself and those who selflessly love you the most.

If you read this today or ten years from now, know that you are loved more than you know.

Step out of your fear and insecurities.

Reject the lie that you are worthless, not good enough.

You are amazing.

Yes, you

Greatness awaits you.

Go get it.

I appreciate each reader of these words and thank God for the blessing you are in my life.

Always and in all ways.

Your true colors are more beautiful than any rainbow.

Inside and out!

PERSPECTIVE

Dear God: Thank you for the amazing gift of perspective that sees mountains as ant hills to be stepped over!

A little perspective goes a long way when facing difficulties.

I used to have panic attacks.

I was once passive-aggressive and avoided conflict because I was a desperate people pleaser.

And often in my endeavors to avoid conflict I created more than I imagined.

Likewise in my attempts to people please I inadvertently hurt people unintentionally.

One day it finally sank in.

"I am not created for the happiness of others. I am not equipped nor responsible for anyone's happiness."

I was so concerned with trying to manipulate the happiness of others around me that I overlooked any prospect of my own happiness.

I had to change my perspective. And once I did, guess what happened?

I got my happy and became a joy to be around.

What perspective do you need to change?

Do you see yourself as broke, negating the value of the gifts God gave you?

Do you see yourself as alone when surrounded by opportunities to receive love?

Do you see yourself as a failure because that ONE thing continues to haunt you?

Your gifts outweigh all of the money in the bank.

Use them to walk in your purpose and experience wealth beyond measure.

Seek opportunities to demonstrate love.

Give freely to others and watch the joy bounce back into your life.

Learn the lesson from that one thing that seems to hold on and allow it make you better, not bitter.

Many things in life may be beyond our control.

Perspective? You choose!

You have the ability to reverse your thought process.

Start by turning mountains into anthills.

Perspective is your friend. Embrace it.

And watch God work.

LIFE

Dear God: Thank you for granting me another day. I am grateful and promise to never stop trying to be better. Forgive my sins.

People die daily.

Before I hit send on this post, someone, somewhere will no longer be among the living.

We all expect to die one day, yet when it happens, we are devastated. Why?

Because we were created to live. What is our response to death?

Grief, mourning and in some cases a desire to carry out a legacy that was cut short.

But, we know that people die daily.

Why not maintain the same spirit of introspection every day?

Because we forget.

We forget that tomorrow is not promised.

We forget that we were born with gifts for the sole purpose of sharing them.

We forget that we may never see our loved ones again. We forget that we are worthy of receiving love.

Celebrate those in your life as often as you can.

Embrace those who celebrate you and welcome them into your heart and life.

And don't forget to remember. Remember that trouble doesn't last always.

Remember that you are loved and appreciated by many whom are not able to show you the depths of their emotion.

Remember that you are royalty and deserve a lifetime of love, joy and happiness.

And most of all: Remember that you are alive so that you can love.

For as long as you can.

MOUNTAINS

Dear God: Thank you for perspective and the assurance that even if mountains are not to be moved, you will help us climb them.

We all know someone who has gone from praising God to blaming God once a mountain appears.

Not every mountain will be cast into the sea.

Not every mountain is intended to be moved. Sometimes, we need to dig in and climb.

Instead of asking how, we constantly ask how long and why, wallowing in distress.

Sometimes, as we are standing in front of a mountain and attempt to go around it, we encounter another.

At some point to reach our destination either the mountain has to be moved or we need to climb it.

Of course, our first thought is that our faith can move the mountain. What if God doesn't want it moved?

What if he wants us to climb the mountain?

There are many people unjustly disappointed in God because they are waiting on him to move a mountain.

But, God is waiting for them to climb it!

Many people are not hearing from God and assume he has left.

Nope.

You aren't listening. There's a message even in silence.

Many times we claim to be looking for the answer when all we want is a way out.

We want the mountain cast into the sea.

Nope.

Too many of us are waiting on God and have missed his message because he's not answering the way we want him to!

Stop looking at every mountain, expecting it to be cast into the sea.

Stop asking God how long that mountain is going to be there while you sit on your hands!

Get up in the silence!

Climb the mountain!

God's got your back. I

If you slip a time or two trust him to pick you up!

Some people spend a lifetime standing in front of the same mountain, year after year, waiting on a "word".

Stop thinking you need to always ask other folks what God is saying.

Ask him!

And if he doesn't give you peace to know the mountain will be moved, in the silence CLIMB.

PERMISSION

Dear God: Remind me daily that your voice is what matters most. Your stamp of approval is all I need.

There's greatness inside of you.

Yet some people won't let you be great.

They belittle the dream that God has placed in your heart even as it rages like a furnace buried in the pit of your soul seeking expression.

The simple truth is: You are already great.

It matters not that your family, friends or even your boss can't comprehend the success God has intended for you.

Your path to greatness is unique and at times might feel like a long crawl on a short road.

Learn how to dismiss the small voices in your head.

"Who do you think you are?"
Reply: I am the one God has chosen for just this purpose.

"You are not smart enough to do this."
Reply: God grants wisdom even to the foolish if they seek it. "

You can't afford that dream house!"
Reply: My Heavenly Father is the landlord of the earth.

"I don't know why you always try to do too much!"
Reply: Because what God has for me is for me. It's not for everyone to understand.

Push self-doubt so far back that there is no longer room for it.

Go be great.
You don't need a permission slip for that.

The moment God planted the dream in your heart, he signed off on it and gave you the green light to go.

And that's what matters most.

FIRES

Dear God: Please give me the faith of Daniel and his comrades. Help me to know that you are there, even AS the fires blaze higher!

There are times in life when it seems that all should be going well, but something is horribly wrong.

It may be that we have finally walked away from previous behaviors or relationships.

It may be that we have finally taken a leap of faith and gotten closer to God's plan for us.

No matter our race, creed, color or social status, fire will come at some point in our lives.

When fire strikes, it's never at a convenient time.

Fires show up unexpectedly and are unwelcome.

But once the fire starts, we have to decide if we will stand firm on God's promises or permit the fire to ravage our faith.

Someone who is reading this is experiencing fire so hot, they don't know if they can go on.

Someone reading this is so close to another person's fire, they are afraid they will be singed by association.

Whatever its, whoever you are, I beg of you: hold on.

It's not over until God says so.

There was a time when three men were thrown into a literal fire - a blazing oven.

Daniel's friends, Hananiah, Mishael and Azariah.

You may know the latter three as Shadrach, Meschach and Abednego but that was not who they were.

They were given Babylonian names.

1) When going through the fire - know whom you are.

Don't ever step out of your identity.

These four young men were chosen.

The Bible describes them as "Israelites from the royal family and nobility—young men who were healthy and handsome."

As well as "intelligent and well-educated, good prospects for leadership positions in the government, perfect specimens!"

2) No one is exempt from going through the fire.

These young men were gifted by God.

"God gave these four young men knowledge and skill in both books and life. In addition, Daniel was gifted in understanding all sorts of visions and dreams."

3) God's anointing over your life does not exclude you from fires.

A death sentence was decreed over these four young men because of the ineptitude of other people.

Why?

The King asked for something to be done that had never been done before:

He wanted someone to not only interpret his dream - they had to tell him what his dream was.

When his Babylon fortunetellers could not do it, he killed them.

He then issued a death decree for all wise men.

"When the death warrant was issued, Daniel and his companions were included. They also were marked for execution."

4) Sometimes our fires come because of other people who have nothing to do with us.

When Daniel found out what was going on, he "went to the King and asked for a little time so that he could interpret the dream."

Then, he asked his companions "to pray to the God of heaven for mercy in solving this mystery so that the four of them wouldn't be killed."

5) Even when we don't understand the reason for the fire, we must continue to pray.

God revealed to Daniel the dream and the interpretation.
When the King asked if he could really tell him his dream, Daniel said Nope. But, God can.

6) Realize your limitations in the fire. Give God the glory even in the midst of it.

After Daniel publicly acknowledged God and gave him the dream and meaning, the King was humbled.

"Your God is beyond question the God of all gods, the Master of all kings."
"
And he solves all mysteries, I know, because you've solved this mystery."

7) God is able to unravel the deepest mysteries surrounding your fires.

But, it wasn't over.

Daniel got promoted to a very high position and at his request, so were his friends.

Still, not over.

That same King later built a gold statue.

He decreed that everyone should bow down or be thrown into a "roaring furnace."

Fire.

When Daniel's companions did not bow down, who do you think told the King?

Babylonian fortunetellers.

8) If you think all of your enemies are destroyed, think again. the enemy is always seeking to devour you.

The Bible doesn't say, but I can only imagine how they felt about Daniel and his friends.

We don't know if they were new fortunetellers or remnants of survivors from the King's decree.

It could be that they felt the favor Daniel and the others had been unfair.

Maybe they were jealous because Daniel gave his friends a hook up.

Perhaps they wanted to do something to endear them to the King.

No matter the reason, they eagerly stepped up at the chance to put Daniel's friends in hellfire.

"These men are ignoring you, O king. They don't respect your gods and they won't worship the gold statue you set up."

9) People who don't like what you stand for will always eagerly serve you up to fire.

So, the King gave them another chance.

He then asked: "Who is the god who can rescue you from my power?"

Say what?

When Daniel told him his dream and interpreted it, what did the King say?

"Your God is beyond question the God of all gods, the Master of all kings."

His friends served that same God.

10) People who are selfish have a short memory when it comes to any good you have done.

Daniel's friends replied:

"Your threat means nothing to us. If you throw us in the fire, the God we serve can rescue us from your roaring furnace and anything else..."
"
But even if he doesn't, it wouldn't make a bit of difference, O king. We still wouldn't serve your gods or worship the gold statue you set up."

You can read the entire account in Daniel Chapters 1-3, but here's the point:

The faith of those men was so strong that they realized it might not have been the will of God to spare them from the fire.

Yet, they were spared and escaped a fiery death.

They came through without even the scent of smoke on their bodies.

But, the strong men who delivered them tied up into the fire, died from the flames.

Know this: When God brings you through something, he brings you through whole.

God never brings people through a fire injured.

Never.

When Jesus was resurrected, he was whole.

When Lazarus came back to life, he was whole.

And as for anyone who serves you up in the fire?

God will deal with them in ways you can't imagine.

This fire you are experiencing won't last always.

It will be put out.

It will be extinguished.

Don't stop praising God in the midst of the fire.

The higher the flames rage, increase the intensity of your praise.

No matter what.

The stronger the calling on your life, the stronger the fire.

Don't give up.

There may be some who fan the flames of the fires in your life.

Surround yourself with those who are pushing you closer to God.

And leave it to God to deal with the fires.

HUSBANDS

Dear God: Cause us to seek your word, not mere Bible "stories" to govern our relationship with you and others.

From the time I was a teenager I've heard single women praying to God for their Boaz.

But, should every single woman be praying for a Boaz?

Not just on this occasion, I beg of you, read your Bible, and get the full account.

Unexpectedly, Ruth loses her husband in death.

Ruth decided never to leave her mother in law and insisted on going back with Naomi to her homeland.

She lost her husband in death and then had to forsake her homeland to go to a foreign land to meet Boaz.

But, there is more.

In those days, it was a dishonor not to carry on the family name by producing offspring.

A kinsmen "inherited" the responsibility for a widowed family member.

The family member who was closest decided, he didn't want the responsibility.

Long story short, Boaz stepped up after another man declined.

Although another kinsman was responsible for her, he decided not to live up to his responsibility.

Now, I'm not trying to omit the romance from the story - read it in the Bible, but, I think Ruth contains lessons for us.

1). Boaz was the second husband of Ruth, after she lost her first in death.

If you've never been married, are you really praying for a Boaz?

Do you want to lose your first husband to get to the second one?

2). Boaz was the man who redeemed Ruth, he foreshadowed Christ as a savior.

What are expecting a man to save you from?

Do you want to be picked over and rejected before you get married?

3). Boaz became Ruth's husband out of obligation to his family, he was related to her husband.

Is that what you are praying for?

Are you praying specifically for Boaz or a redeemer?

Are you more interested in the fact that Boaz provided for all her needs?

Then, pray for a good provider, someone who believes in God's principle of working so that you may eat.

You don't need to survive the loss of a first husband in order to get a good one.

When I think of Esther and how the king wined and dined and pampered the women he courted, I might want that, but, I don't want him!

He disrespected his first Queen Vashti by asking her to dance for his drunken friends!

I don't want that.

Choose your words wisely.

Do you want a man like Boaz who honored the law?

Or do you want everything about Boaz?

Are you willing to walk the path that Ruth walked to get your Boaz?

It's like people who see those at the height of their career, but don't know their story.

Never go for the glory, without accepting that there is a story.

And it might not be so pretty.

I don't have a name for my future husband.

But, he will be mine and I will be his.

Most importantly, I am willing to wait for God to manifest him to me.

That road might not be so pretty.

But it will be worth it in the end.

Be careful what you ask for.

You just might get it.

If you've never read the entire book of Ruth, why not today?

Those four chapters that will change your perspective.

DISTRACTIONS

Dear God: Thank you for exposing and removing the enemy's distractions from my life.

Have you ever noticed that just as God is moving, distractions appear in your life?

Pay attention to the chatter around you, but be aware that sometimes chatter is just chatter.

When we become extremely busy, we need to make sure that we don't confuse busyness with business.

Our sense of urgency should never be predicated upon someone else's.

Never lose sight of the specific plan God has for you, even as you help others.

Joseph got distracted.

For years, God was preparing him for his purpose.

Joseph's training included:
Ridicule
Enemies
Slavery
Imprisonment
Distractions

When Joseph thought he had enough and was ready, God shut him down.

How?

By promoting and demoting others right in front of him.

Although Joseph was instrumental in getting the cupbearer and baker to the next level, it wasn't his time.

Why?

God wasn't done processing him.

When he interpreted the cupbearer's dream, because it was favorable, Joseph tried to insert himself into it.

He told the cupbearer to "remember" him as if God who provided him with the revelation of the dream had forgotten him.

But to the Baker, who was destined for execution, he said nothing.

1). God is always making a way for us. Even when we think we are forgotten.
2). God may lead us to manifest a dream in someone else long before he fulfills ours.
3). Even when God helps us reveal the dreams of others, some of them will die and not flourish.
In the end, Joseph was promoted in such a way that he was described as the only person for the job.

What about us?

Are we distracted when God sends us to facilitate someone else's dream?

Do we minimize the value of our own process instead of trusting God's timing?

Just as Joseph did, there will be those who see the favorable outcome God has planned for you.

They become distracted and attempt to get you to promote their agendas in concert or even ahead of yours.

"Remember me..."

"Don't forget about me..."

Know this: Even if you tried, you could not get them any closer to their dream than God allows.

Don't become distracted by the move of God in someone else's life.

Don't allow others to distract you from your process.

After all, if we diss the traction we are making, we run the risk of distancing ourselves from God's plan for us.

And that distance may be enough to cause our dreams to be killed.

Just like the Baker.

INFLUENCERS

Dear God: Thank you for the ability, desire, and the discernment to seek out wise counsel. I appreciate those in my circle of trust.

There are times when we need to seek answers to things that will move us forward in greatness.

Others times the answer is standing right in front of us.

But in some instances "two heads are better than one."

Invest the time in vetting the people in your life.

Continually examine those who speak to you and over you.

There is a difference.

Those who speak over your life have the ability to speak into your life.

Not everyone has earned that privilege. Why give it away so freely?

If you have not granted permission for anyone to speak over and into your life with authority I urge you to do two things:

1). Examine those who are currently attempting to do so. Deny, revoke access and establish appropriate boundaries to those undeserving.
2). Seek out and align yourself with those who can be trusted with the power of their words in your life.

Who should you grant access to speak over and into your life?

Who are your ideal influencers?

Those who will do these three key things:
1). Be completely honest with you.
2). Be completely honest with themselves.

3). Honor the words that God has already spoken over you.

Anyone else should only be speaking to you.

They are gum bumpers who don't have the chops to take a bite into your life.

We can't allow people to speak recklessly over us and then wonder why we don't have peace and joy.

Seek out genuine prayer warriors who eagerly enter into battle on your behalf.

How do you identify them?

1). God hears and answers their prayers.
2). Their "answered" prayer is made equally manifest in the lives of others as well as their own.
3). They are humble in their gift and not drunk with power.
4). They intercede on behalf of others unprompted, absent of pomp and circumstance in private.
5). They do not boast in answered prayer. They glorify God in answered prayer.
6). They do not say the words "God told me to tell you" or "Thus saith the Lord" in attempts to manipulate you.
7). They acknowledge they are flawed and will struggle, since their main desire is to please God.
8). Not every "word" they deliver is a revelation. God will use them to confirm aloud what he whispered in your heart privately.

And I personally believe the final two are the most important.

It's my measure of whom to allow to speak over and into my life:

9). They are immersed in the Word of God and bathe in prayer.

You cannot hear from God if you aren't listening.

10). Someone is speaking over and into their lives!

Trust me on this: When God gives you a dream, he will send you a team.

Don't permit people to speak nightmares over your dreams.

PROVISION

Dear God: Thank you for going ahead of us to prepare a way, so that when we catch up, greatness will occur.

It's so easy to get frustrated while waiting on God.

But truth be told, more often than not we are not waiting on God.

He is waiting on us.

Think of God's plan for us as an unlimited debit card.

Not credit that needs to be repaid.

If we don't swipe the card and avail ourselves of the benefits, we will continue to wait.

What are we not doing that God is waiting on so he can release his debit card of blessings to us?

Have we put limits on God?

Have we said in our head "I'm not going to ask God for that?"

Or how many times have we half-heartedly asked, not really expecting to receive?

What's the point of having a debit card in the supermarket, with the ability to purchase anything you want and walk away empty-handed?

Faith requires work.

It doesn't mean to simply ask.

Are you ready for what God has already prepared for you?

Too many folks are waiting on God for money and not realizing the blessing of provision!

Are we like the widow of Zarepath?

When Elijah went to her and asked her to feed him, she said "we only have enough food for me and my son to eat and then die".

Read the full account in 1 Kings 17.

Because God honored Elijah, she was blessed.

Because she was obedient, she was blessed.

Notice that God gave an abundance.

Overflow.

No cash required.

But, even after her food was replenished and needs met beyond measure, she challenged God.

Her son died.

And she asked Elijah if he had come to curse her!

The very woman who was in expectation of her son's death before the Man of God caused her to be blessed.

Have we turned on God and his people when it got tough?

Do we forget the times that he has provided in our time of need?

The proof of the miracle of provision was still in her house, yet, she was angry with God.

And once again, God used Elijah. He brought her son back to life.

Again, she was blessed because of Elijah!

Here's the thing: Some of us have been indirect recipients of the blessing of God.

We are swiping someone else's debit card of unlimited blessings.

Today, I challenge you to get your own!

Unlimited blessings! No payment plan. No incurring debt.

But, are we ready for what God has prepared for us?

Has our pro vision shown us that all of our actions result in consequences?

What are we choosing to swipe the card for?

And what are we expecting to receive in return?

If we seek greatness, do we conduct ourselves with excellency in every area of our life?

We cannot ask God to set an elaborate table with filet mignon and show up to the table with plastic cutlery.

Are we ready?

What will you do differently today, to prepare for what you are asking God for?

Conduct yourself today as if you have already received God's promises, because the truth is - they are waiting for you.

Become a vision pro so that you can excel in recognizing God's provision for you.